CW00499016

VICTORIA TO BROMLEY SOUTH

Vic Mitchell and Keith Smith

First published February 1992

ISBN 0 906520 98 3

Typesetting   - Barbara Mitchell
Design   - Deborah Goodridge

Published by Middleton Press
              Easebourne Lane
              Midhurst
              West Sussex
              GU29 9AZ
              Tel: (0730) 813169

Printed & bound by Biddles Ltd,
              Guildford and Kings Lynn

CONTENTS

MAPS

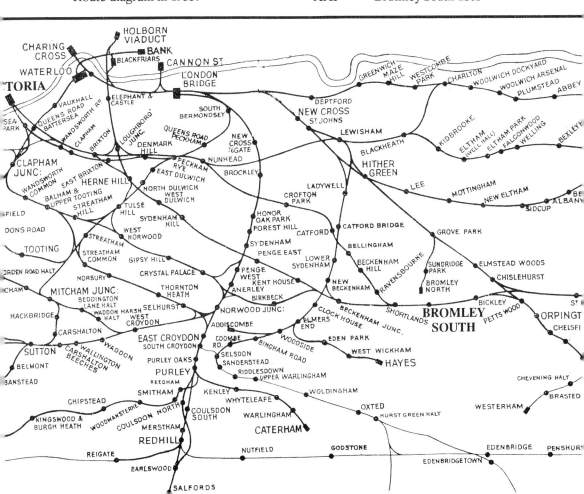

ACKNOWLEDGEMENTS

Many of those mentioned in the photographic attributions have given us much assistance, as have J.H.Aston, R.M.Casserley, Dr.E.Course, G.Croughton, K.Deakin, J.N. Faulkner, Mrs V.Jurczyniki, J.R.W.Kirkby, N.Langridge, A.Ll.Lambert, D.Lovett (NSE), R.Randell, D.Salter, E.Staff, N.Stanyon and our ever helpful wives. To all these, we express our deep gratitude.

GEOGRAPHICAL SETTING

The Victoria - Wandsworth Road section is on the alluvium laid down by the River Thames, the route then crossing the gravels of the river terraces cut by the Thames and its tributaries. It then tunnels through London Clay under Sydenham Hill. This U-shaped ridge of clay encircles South London and has presented problems to railway engineers on most routes into the capital.

The line then crosses the flood plain gravel of the River Pool and its tributaries, entering the pebbles and sand of the Blackheath Beds at Bromley South.

All maps in this album are to the scale of 25" to 1 mile, unless otherwise noted.

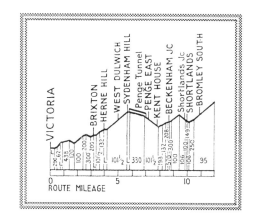

HISTORICAL BACKGROUND

In 1858 The East Kent Railway started running between Strood and Faversham but in 1859 it changed its name to London, Chatham & Dover Railway, with the intention of linking all three places.

In the London area, the West End of London & Crystal Palace Railway opened between Wandsworth and Crystal Palace via Balham in 1856 and was extended to Battersea Pier (misleadingly named Pimlico which is north of the River) on 29th May 1858. On 3rd May 1858, an eastward extension to Shortlands (then named Bromley) took place, this being followed on 5th July by the line to Southborough Road (now Bickley), with one intermediate station (now Bromley South). This latter section was built by the Crays Company and was leased by the LCDR after their line between Strood and Bickley was opened on 3rd December 1860.

The WELCPR became part of the London, Brighton & South Coast Railway and so the LCDR planned its own independent and more direct route to the West End, via Herne Hill. It was opened north of Herne Hill on 25th August 1862 and southwards on 1st July 1863. Thereafter the LCDR ceased to run via Crystal Palace and Balham.

Meanwhile, the Victoria Station & Pimlico Railway Co. had built its short but expensive line in 1859-60 and offered terminal facilities north of the Thames to the LBSCR, LCDR and GWR (whose trains first had to cross the river at Chelsea). Victoria opened for LBSCR services on 1st October 1860 and for LCDR trains on 3rd December following. As a result of disputes, separate stations were provided,

PASSENGER SERVICES

The following notes cover local trains only and refer to down services between Victoria and Bromley South. They omit details of the intensive service between Wandsworth Road and Brixton provided until 3rd April 1916 by trains from Victoria or Kensington to Ludgate Hill or North London destinations.

By way of example from the 1860s, the 1869 timetable showed 17 weekday trains (with three additional services between North London and Beckenham) and 12 on Sundays. By 1881 the figures were 17 and 7 respectively. Between 1873 and 1881, there was a slip coach service at Beckenham from one down train. There was a similar facility at Herne Hill from an up afternoon Maidstone train between 1881 and 1924. By 1890, there were over 40 weekday trains on offer, the service increasing steadily until electrification in 1925.

The basic initial electric service comprised trains every 20 minutes from Victoria and every 20 minutes from Holborn Viaduct, giving six trains per hour south of Herne Hill. Most terminated at Orpington, having called at all stations. Steam trains continued to provide a fast service to Bromley South.

By 1945 the interval was increased to 60 minutes during the middle of the day, reverting to half hourly by 1948, a frequency which still applied in 1991.

the eastern one for LCDR traffic coming into use on 25th August 1862.

Trains to Battersea Pier, and later Victoria, passed *under* the London & South Western Railway's main line to Waterloo but this resulted in a steep climb to the Grosvenor Bridge over the Thames. Following widening of the bridge, a new route passing *over* the LSWR came into use on 20th December 1866, joining the original line at Factory Junction. It was triple track and included a station at Battersea Park Road, opened on 1st May 1867.

The LCDR's other London main line from Herne Hill was completed to the City in 1864-66, as was its branch to Crystal Palace (High Level). These and the LCDR's other suburban lines are described in our *Holborn Viaduct to Lewisham* and *Crystal Palace and Catford Loop* albums. A comprehensive history of the company can be found in Adrian Gray's *London, Chatham & Dover Railway*, available from Middleton Press.

The LBSCR's South London Line between Victoria and London Bridge ran roughly parallel to the LCDR between Victoria and Brixton, services commencing on most of the route on 1st May 1867.

From 1st January 1899, the LCDR and the South Eastern Railway were operated by a joint managing committee, the combined systems soon becoming known as the South Eastern and Chatham Railway. This in turn became part of the Southern Railway in 1923. Electrification of the route followed on 12th July 1925, when the Catford Loop and the lines to Holborn Viaduct and Orpington were also electrified.

The subsequent historical event of note was nationalisation in 1948, when British Railways was formed.

VICTORIA

1. The approach to Victoria had to be covered with glass in order to placate local residents and landowners, notably the Duke of Westminster. The roof demolition was completed in about 1907. The curious signalling was controlled from a recess in the wall on the right. Note the third rail provided for GWR trains and the variable number of signal spectacle glasses. (Railway Magazine)

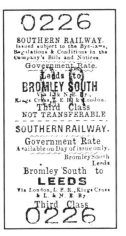

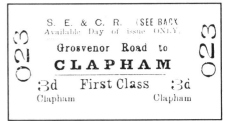

2. Known as the "Hole-in-the-Wall" this LBSCR "box" worked signals and points from 1860 until 1866, when the second bridge was completed. A new "Hole-in-the Wall" then came into use on the LCDR side, the frame here being extended piecemeal. It even contained wooden quadrant plates and remained in use until 1920 as a reminder of the unorthodoxy and ingenuity of the LCDR. (Railway Magazine)

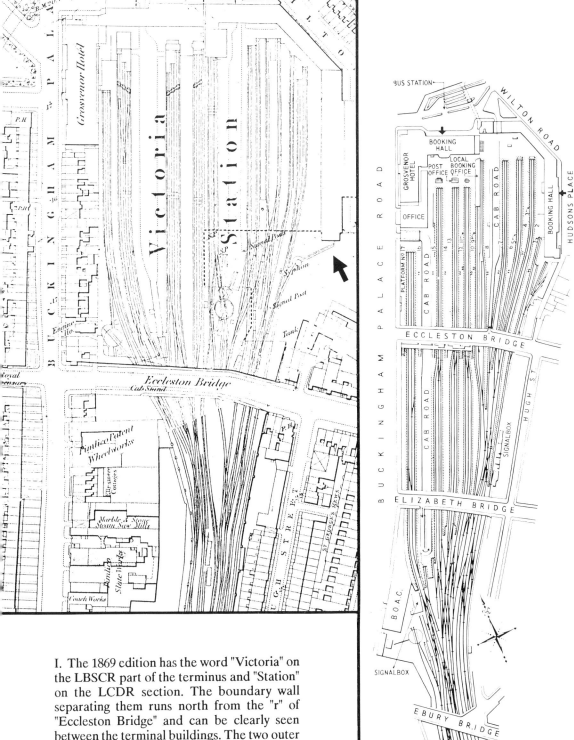

I. The 1869 edition has the word "Victoria" on the LBSCR part of the terminus and "Station" on the LCDR section. The boundary wall separating them runs north from the "r" of "Eccleston Bridge" and can be clearly seen between the terminal buildings. The two outer pairs of tracks of the nine LCDR lines were of mixed gauge to accommodate the GWR broad gauge stock. On the right is the arrangement in 1960. (Railway Magazine)

3. On the right is the LBSCR station with its fine 1880 carriage cover, now in use at Hove. In the background is the Grosvenor Hotel, the only building in this view still standing in 1991. The former LCDR offices (left) were rebuilt in 1909. The notices are worthy of study. (Lens of Sutton)

4. The original mean structures erected for both companies were replaced by buildings worthy of being described as the "West End" termini. Note that the GWR received large letters despite its limited services. It remained joint lessee of this side of the station until 1932. (Lens of Sutton)

5. New offices are in the background but the scene is dominated by the fine twin spans of the LCDR train shed, which is still in use today.

6. To the left of the H class 0-6-0 is a GWR 2-4-0 "Metro" tank. The GWR operated broad gauge services from 1863 until 1866 to and from Reading and Windsor, but most trains were standard gauge, operating to and from

The locomotive is displaying its condensing pipe, used when working in the tunnels in the City. Great Northern Railway trains from Barnet ran via Loughborough Junction to these platforms from 1st March 1868 until 1st October 1907. (Lens of Sutton)

Southall until 1915. In 1864, there were slip coaches from Bristol and in 1905-6 Birkenhead -Dover coaches were shunted at Victoria, having been slipped at Southall. A Birmingham service started in 1910. (D.Cullum coll.)

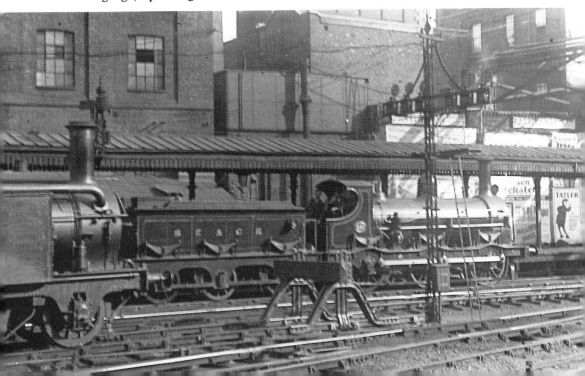

7. The transfer of horse boxes from one passenger train to another was one of the functions of the station pilot. This duty is being performed by SECR no. 560 (ex-LCDR no. 101), an 0-4-4T of 1875 scrapped in 1925. (Lens of Sutton)

8. Viewed from the cab road from Eccleston Bridge, SER class B1 4-4-0 no. A449 stands on one of the tracks electrified in 1925. In June 1922, the platforms were renumbered and altered, no. 1 being on the right thereafter, instead of the left. The archway in the distance is the one seen in picture 4. (Lens of Sutton)

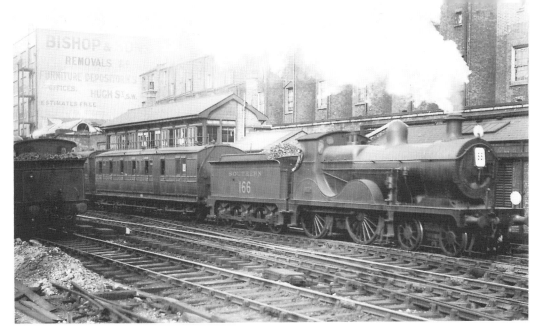

9. Behind E class no. A166 is Victoria "A" Box, which opened on 4th January 1920 and replaced the second "Hole-in-the-Wall". The prefix letters on locomotives were in use between 1923 and 1931, "A" usually indicating Ashford origin. The leading coach is an ex-LCDR eight-wheeled 3rd brake.
(Lens of Sutton)

10. "King Arthur" class no. 801 *Sir Meliot de Logres* waits to depart in 1936, a low level roof having been added by then as train lengths were increasing. In January 1924, an archway was cut in the wall between the stations and in 1990 work commenced on widening this to improve circulation between the two concourses.
(C.R.L.Coles)

The LBSCR side of Victoria station is described and fully illustrated in our *Victoria to East Croydon* album.

11. The unusual three-position semaphore signals dated from January 1920, as did electrical operation of points. Also visible are the three-position shunt signals, unique to Victoria. These were of American manufacture and were replaced in 1939 when Victoria "B" box was closed. The photograph dates from 1925 when the "King Arthurs" were new. All the headcodes show Dover Marine via Orpington. (Lens of Sutton)

12. A Pullman boat train to Dover was introduced in November 1924 but it was not named the "Golden Arrow" until May 1929, although the French connection was so named (Flèche D'or) in 1926. The service was suspended between September 1939 and April 1946. No. 21C119 (later named *Bideford*) is ready for departure with this all 1st class luxury train in 1946. (C.R.L.Coles)

13. On the evening of 9th December 1949, the up "Golden Arrow" was crossing from the up main to the up relief line on which no. 34085 *501 Squadron* was travelling slowly. The driver of this engine had misread the signals. Subsequently the 6.40pm Victoria to East Croydon electric collided with the derailed engine.

Eight people were injured. Second class Pullmans were introduced in 1949 and the "Golden Arrow" ceased to be all-Pullman in 1954. The service ended on 30th September 1972 but Victoria continues to be the principal departure station for surface travellers to mainland Europe. (British Rail)

"GOLDEN ARROW"
PULLMAN SERVICE
between
LONDON and PARIS
EVERY DAY IN EACH DIRECTION

Miles	1 & 2 Cl. Luxe.						1 & 2 Cl. Luxe.
	p.m.						p.m.
—	1* 0	dep.		LONDON (Victoria) ... arr.	↑		6*30
72	2*38 3*10	arr. dep.	} ...	Folkestone Harbour ...	{ dep. arr.		... ...
—	... ...	arr. dep.	} ...	Dover Marine ...	{ dep. arr.		4*58 4*23
103	4*40 Br.T. 5 40 Fr.T. 6 2	arr. arr. dep.	} ...	Calais Maritime ...	{ dep. dep. arr.		3* 5 Br.T. 4 5 Fr.T. 3 45
288	9 44	↓ arr.		PARIS (Nord) ...	dep.		12 25

*—One hour later from 17th April, 1955
Br.T.—British Time.   **Fr.T.**—French Time (One hour in advance of British Time from 3rd October, 1954, to 16th April, 1955 inclusive).

FARES (*liable to alteration*).

	1st Class £ s. d.	2nd Class Rail, 1st Class Steamer £ s. d.
LONDON to PARIS ... ... SINGLE	7 6 0	6 4 6
	(available 1 month)	
RETURN	14 2 0	12 0 0
	(available 2 months)	

	£ s. d.	£ s. d.
Supplement for Reservation of Pullman seats on both sides of the Channel	1 7 2	– 18 8
		in each direction

INCLUSIVE PULLMAN MEAL TICKETS

Pullman tickets, including the cost of meals (as well as gratuities) in the "Golden Arrow" Pullman Cars on both sides of the Channel, can be obtained at time of booking. Ask for details.

For Tickets, Seat Reservations, Cabin Accommodation, etc., apply to :—

LONDON : Continental Enquiry Office, British Railways (Southern Region), Victoria Station, S.W.1 (in Hudson's Place ; adjacent to Platform No. 1) ; or to British Railways Travel Centre, Lower Regent Street, S.W.1 ; or principal Travel Agencies.

PARIS : British Railways' Office, 12, Boulevard de la Madeleine; or principal Travel Agencies.

October 1954

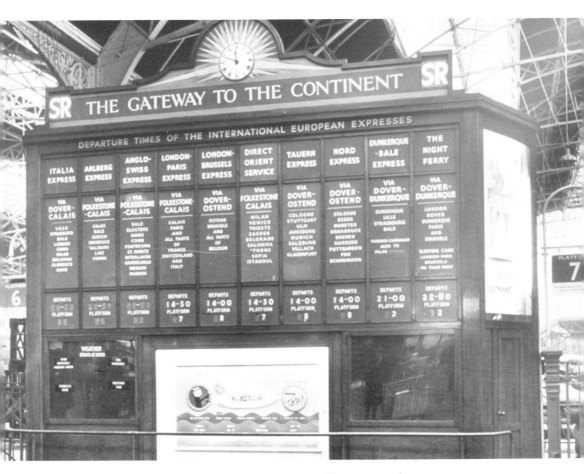

14. Three separate manually operated indicators were in use from 1928 until 1971. In addition to that shown, there was one nearby for Kent and some suburban services, and another near platform 12 for Central Division trains. A completely new system was installed in April 1988, costing £1.7m. (British Rail)

15. This southward view from the 1950s includes Eccleston Bridge, principal stopping place of one of the railway's competitors, Green Line Coaches. Also featured are the well protected platforms 7 and 8, both over 300 yds long. On the left is the 174-lever Eastern signal box, which controlled this side of the station until 13th May 1979. Soon afterwards, the Victoria Panel at Clapham Junction took over this area and the tracks were redesignated. The down slow became down Chatham fast; down fast became up Chatham fast; up fast became down Chatham slow and up branch became up Chatham slow. (Lens of Sutton)

October 1954

"THE NIGHT FERRY"
THROUGH SLEEPING CAR SERVICE
(1st and 2nd Class)

LONDON—PARIS
via
DOVER—DUNKERQUE

FERRY STEAMERS ... { "HAMPTON FERRY" "SHEPPERTON FERRY" "TWICKENHAM FERRY" "SAINT-GERMAIN"

NIGHTLY IN EACH DIRECTION (except 25th December)

*9 0 p.m.	dep.	LONDON (Victoria) ... ...arr.	9 10 a.m.
9 0 a.m.	arr.	PARIS (Nord) ... ... dep.	9 45 p.m.

Restaurant Cars, London-Dover and Dunkerque-Paris, and vice versa.
*—One hour later from 17th April, 1955.

NOTE —Sleeping Car passengers should be at Victoria not later than 30 minutes before the advertised departure time in order to comply with H.M. Customs and Immigration formalities. The French Customs' examination of baggage registered from London to Paris takes place upon arrival at Paris (Nord).

16. Although the last steam hauled "Golden Arrow" left on 11th June 1961 (behind no. 34100 *Appledore*), the train continued, albeit with electric traction. No. E5006 is one of thirteen electric locomotives built for the Kent main line electrification scheme and is seen in September 1962. Platform extensions in 1961 resulted in nos. 3 and 4 being able to accommodate ten cars and nos. 5 and 6 twelve. (C.R.L.Coles)

17. International sleeping cars stand at platform 2, which was always the longest and was further extended in 1961 to receive 18 vehicles. The canopies were also erected at this time. For years, the "Night Ferry" departed at 22.00 and gave the choice of arrival in Paris at 08.40 or Brussels at 09.07. The last departure was on 31st October 1980. (E.Wilmshurst)

18. Electro-diesel no. 73138 stands at platform 5 on 27th June 1982, while its vans were loaded with newspapers. There was also one Mk.I passenger coach in the train which formed the 03.50 to Folkestone. Bulk newspaper traffic ceased in 1988. (J.S.Petley)

19. Having just been drawn into platform 2 with its empty train, London Transport's *Sarah Siddons* waits to leave with a railtour to Folkestone on 21st September 1985. Eccleston Bridge (left) had been reconstructed in 1961 to give a single span over platforms 1-7. Platforms 1 and 2 had received conductor rails by that time. (D.Brown)

GROSVENOR ROAD

20. Approaching Victoria on 11th June 1957, the sleeping cars of the "Night Ferry" are on Grosvenor Bridge while class L1 no. 31788 is at the site of Grosvenor Road station. Behind no. 34017 *Ilfracombe* are international mail vans which were shunted onto the ferry with the sleeping passengers, provided that they were deaf. (P.Hay)

21. The climb from Victoria to Grosvenor Bridge is severe at 1 in 64 and is being tackled by no. 30802 *Sir Durnore* on 13th June 1959, while in charge of the 10.35am Victoria to Ramsgate. On the right are the carriage shed sidings which were not electrified until 1961. (S.C.Nash)

22. On Sunday 5th August 1956, Q class no. 30533 was scheduled to haul the 10.50am to Sheerness-on-Sea, to take some Londoners for a breath of sea air. At that time the track on the right was used for berthing and known as the "Wall Road". It became part of the "down slow" in 1961 and subsequently reverted to a siding. (J.J.Smith)

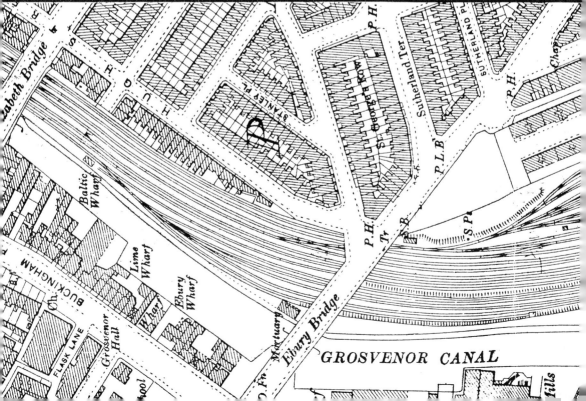

II. The 1894 map marks Grosvenor Road station which was opened on 1st January 1867 for ticket collecting purposes. It was open to the public from 1st November 1870 until 1st April 1907 for LBSCR passengers and from 1st November 1867 until 1st October 1911 for LCDR customers. Most of the Grosvenor Canal has been obliterated except for the part near the church-like sewage pumping house. Part of Victoria station had been built in the canal basin. This southern extremity is still used by barges removing refuse. Initially the bridge carried only two tracks, both mixed gauge. In 1866 an additional bridge was opened, this carrying three mixed gauge lines and two at standard gauge, one of which was for LBSCR services. The combination of tracks varied over the years.

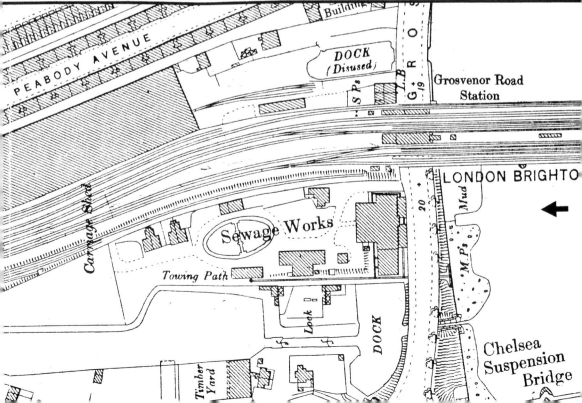

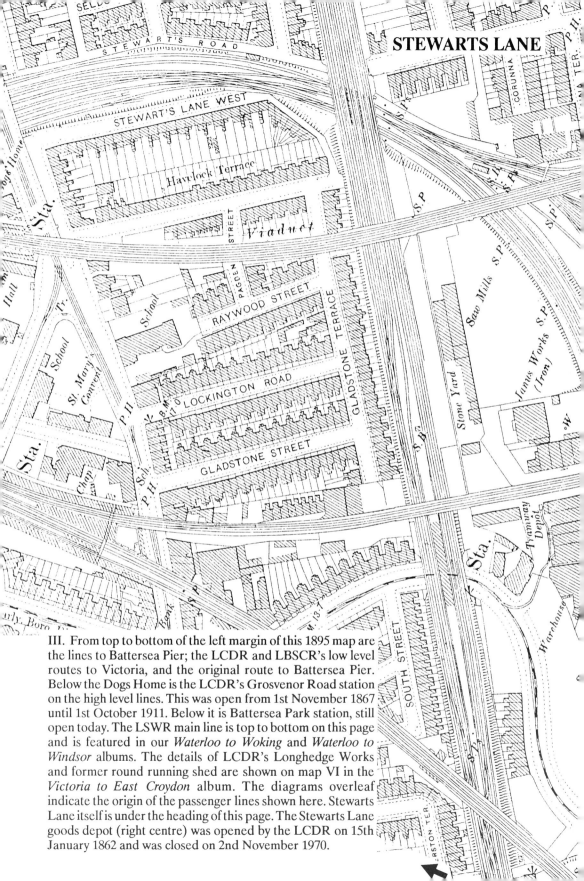

STEWARTS LANE

III. From top to bottom of the left margin of this 1895 map are the lines to Battersea Pier; the LCDR and LBSCR's low level routes to Victoria, and the original route to Battersea Pier. Below the Dogs Home is the LCDR's Grosvenor Road station on the high level lines. This was open from 1st November 1867 until 1st October 1911. Below it is Battersea Park station, still open today. The LSWR main line is top to bottom on this page and is featured in our *Waterloo to Woking* and *Waterloo to Windsor* albums. The details of LCDR's Longhedge Works and former round running shed are shown on map VI in the *Victoria to East Croydon* album. The diagrams overleaf indicate the origin of the passenger lines shown here. Stewarts Lane itself is under the heading of this page. The Stewarts Lane goods depot (right centre) was opened by the LCDR on 15th January 1862 and was closed on 2nd November 1970.

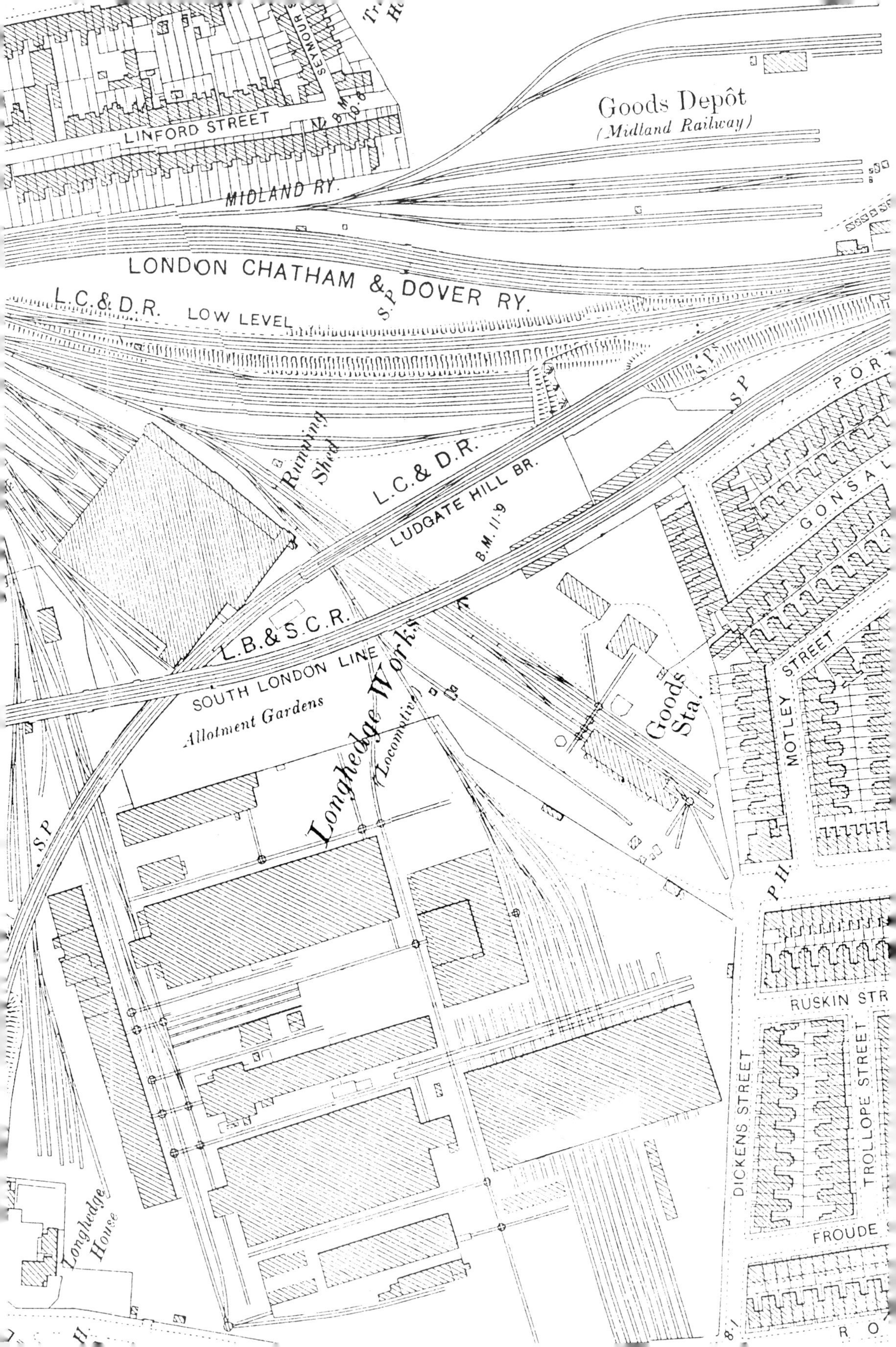

LINFORD STREET

SEYMOUR

B.M. 10·6

MIDLAND RY.

Goods Depôt
(Midland Railway)

LONDON CHATHAM & DOVER RY.

L.C.&D.R. LOW LEVEL

S.P

Running Shed

L.C.&D.R.

LUDGATE HILL BR.

B.M. 11·9

S.P

S.P

POR

GONSAL

L.B.&S.C.R.

SOUTH LONDON LINE

Allotment Gardens

Longhedge Works

(Locomotive)

Goods
Sta.

STREET

MOTLEY STREET

S.P

Longhedge
House

P. H.

RUSKIN STR

DICKENS STREET

TROLLOPE STREET

FROUDE

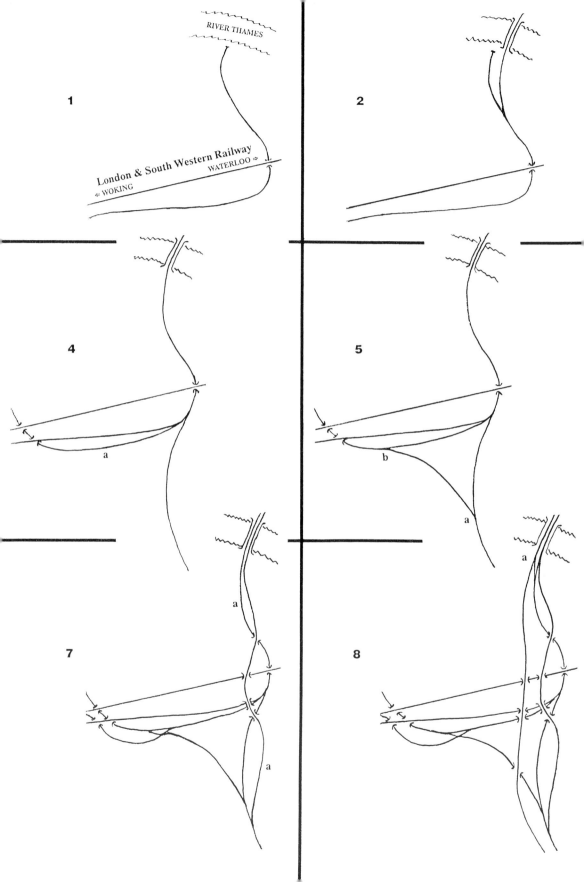

1

RIVER THAMES

London & South Western Railway   WATERLOO ⇨
⇦ WOKING

2

4

a

5

b

a

7

a

a

8

a

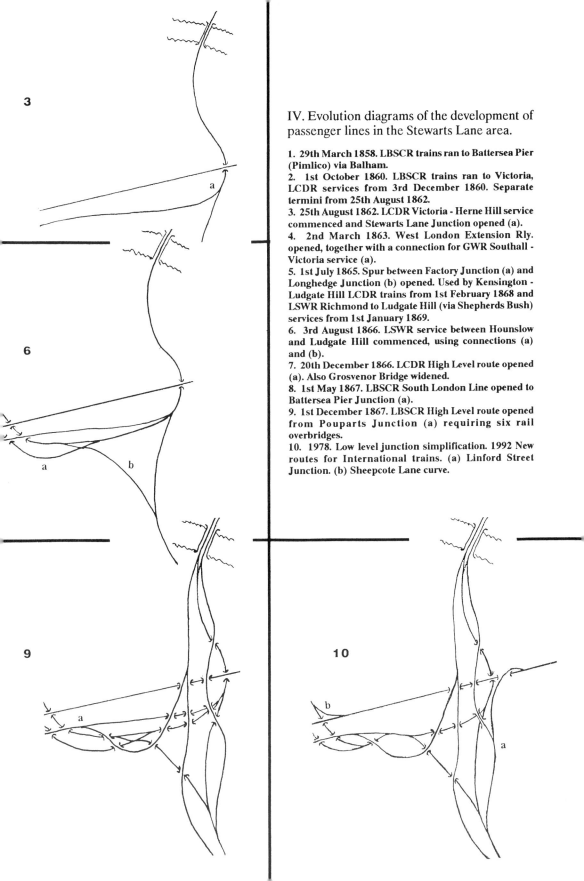

3

6

9

10

IV. Evolution diagrams of the development of passenger lines in the Stewarts Lane area.

1. 29th March 1858. LBSCR trains ran to Battersea Pier (Pimlico) via Balham.
2. 1st October 1860. LBSCR trains ran to Victoria, LCDR services from 3rd December 1860. Separate termini from 25th August 1862.
3. 25th August 1862. LCDR Victoria - Herne Hill service commenced and Stewarts Lane Junction opened (a).
4. 2nd March 1863. West London Extension Rly. opened, together with a connection for GWR Southall - Victoria service (a).
5. 1st July 1865. Spur between Factory Junction (a) and Longhedge Junction (b) opened. Used by Kensington - Ludgate Hill LCDR trains from 1st February 1868 and LSWR Richmond to Ludgate Hill (via Shepherds Bush) services from 1st January 1869.
6. 3rd August 1866. LSWR service between Hounslow and Ludgate Hill commenced, using connections (a) and (b).
7. 20th December 1866. LCDR High Level route opened (a). Also Grosvenor Bridge widened.
8. 1st May 1867. LBSCR South London Line opened to Battersea Pier Junction (a).
9. 1st December 1867. LBSCR High Level route opened from Pouparts Junction (a) requiring six rail overbridges.
10. 1978. Low level junction simplification. 1992 New routes for International trains. (a) Linford Street Junction. (b) Sheepcote Lane curve.

23. The LCDR decided to build a locomotive works near London and to this end purchased the 68 acre Longhedge Farm in 1861. The erecting shops were equipped with this steam powered traverser and 50 locomotives were completed between 1869 and 1904, when constructional work was centred on the former SER works at Ashford.
(W.Palmer/R.C.Riley coll.)

24. A roundhouse was erected as a running shed and opened in February 1862. It was superseded in 1881 by this 16-road shed, which had a staff of 275 by 1902. Note the raised siding to serve the coaling sheds, lower right.
(W.Palmer/R.C.Riley coll.)

25. Another view from the main line viaduct shows the heavily polluted air on 3rd October 1931. The shed was modernised in 1933-34 when it became "Stewarts Lane" instead of "Battersea" and the largest depot on the SR, with up to 170 locomotives. The former LBSCR depot at Battersea Park was closed at this time and the allocation was moved to Stewarts Lane. (H.C.Casserley)

26. In 1925, the SR carried out trials in the yard of Mr.G.Constantinesco's torque converter, which had been constructed in 1923 on the chassis of GWR 0-6-0 no. 395, altered to 2-4-0. Power from a six cylinder petrol engine was via the unwheeled axle, used as a jack shaft. It was shown at the Wembley exhibition in 1924 and at the International Railway Congress in 1925. It is standing close to the arches carrying the South London line, which was operated by overhead 6700 volt AC current at that time. (Lens of Sutton)

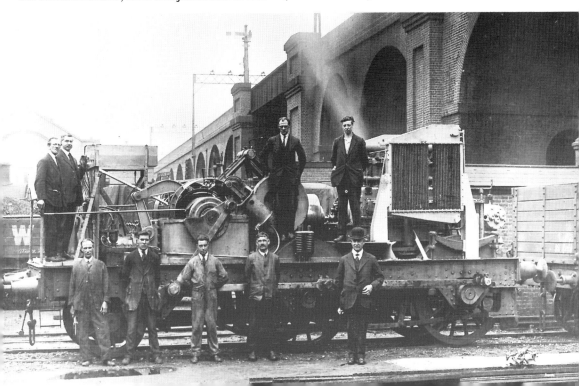

27. Looking north from the locomotive depot on 31st July 1944, we see the former LCDR high level line to Victoria and evidence of recent enemy action. The bridge in the distance carries the Waterloo lines over the Victoria low level tracks, a few yards north of Stewarts Lane Junction, the box being on the extreme right and in use from 1933 until 1980. The staff footbridge partly obscures it. LMS no. 4043 stands on one of the four low level lines on the left. Stewarts Lane passenger station was situated south of the junction and was in use from 1st May 1863 until 1st January 1867. (British Rail)

28. Class C no. 31576 runs off the 1865 spur from Factory Junction at Longhedge Junction on 19th September 1954, with a "Last Day" railtour from Crystal Palace (High Level). It is passing under the ex-LBSCR high level route. (S.C.Nash)

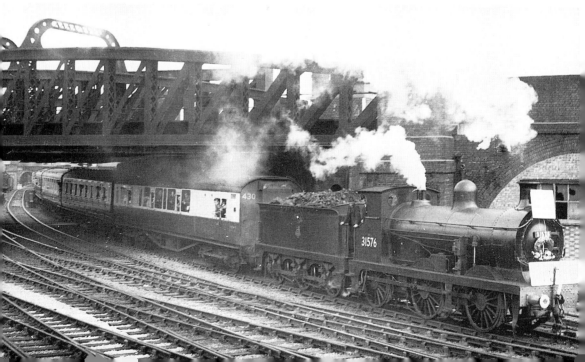

29. The former Longhedge Works was recorded on 20th October 1957 as partial demolition commenced. The P class 0-6-0T is close to the viaduct carrying the South London Line. (R.C.Riley)

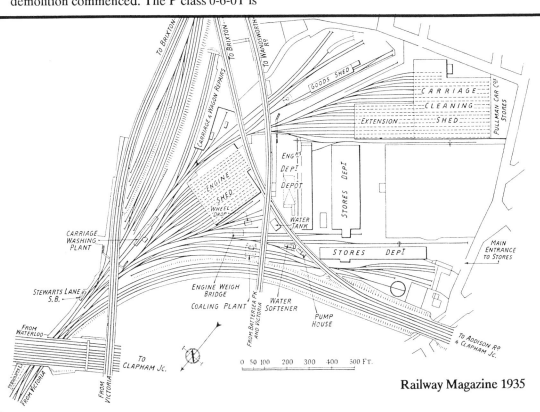

30. Viewed on 10th September 1959, Stewarts Lane still housed a variety of locomotives and did so until steam ceased here in 1963. In the 1950s, the shed turned out immaculate "Merchant Navy" and "Britannia" class Pacifics for the prestigious Pullman and boat trains. From left to right is the water tank, water softener, coaling plant (300 ton capacity) and the span carrying the South London line over the four low level lines from the west. (R.C.Riley)

31. Another 1959 view has the steam shed on the right and the 1865 Ludgate Hill branch on spans in front of the 1867 South London arches. Under them pass the lines to Stewarts Lane Goods Depot. On the left is the new depot for electric locomotives and the low level lines from Factory Junction. (R.C.Riley)

32. A September 1991 picture from the high level line to Victoria reveals that the east wall of the steam shed remained. The carriage washing plant (lower right) is used by Gatwick Express stock which passes under the arch to the right of the crane to reach its depot. (V.Mitchell)

33. Almost continuous with and to the right of the previous picture is the diesel part of the depot, together with the remaining one of four lines between Longhedge and Stewarts Lane Junctions, now known as "Battersea Reversible". In 1991, the depot was renamed "Battersea Stewarts Lane" and described as a marriage of convenience between InterCity and Trainload Construction sectors. The 210 staff care for the Venice Simplon Orient Express, the Gatwick Express fleet, their locomotives, the NSE snow train and 30 engineering vehicles. (V.Mitchell)

FACTORY JUNCTION

34. The junction came into use on 1st July 1865. The first factory to be built on the surrounding farmland was that producing LCDR locomotives and is visible in the left background. This is the scene on 8th June 1952, as the new box nears completion. It remained in use until 17th May 1980 but was still standing in 1991. (Pamlin Prints) ←

L. C. & D. R.
CLAPHAM ROAD
TO (S. 68)
LUDGATE HILL
THIRD CLASS
4d   4d
Available on the day of issue only.
See Other Side.
LUDGATE HILL   LUDGATE HILL
1074 ... 1074

← ■■

35. The high level LCDR route was triple track from the outset but only two were electrified in 1925, as is evident from this view from the mid-1950s of no. 35029 *Ellerman Lines*, now shown in section at the National Railway Museum. On the left are the sidings once used for sorting wagons to and from northern companies but little used since the expansion of Hither Green Yard in 1929-30. (D.Cullum)

36. This is the signalman's view of DEMU no. 1003 when new, on its delivery trip from Eastleigh Works on 27th February 1957. The freight train is standing on the 1862 low level main line to Victoria, prior to shunting. (R.C.Riley)

WANDSWORTH ROAD

V. This map is continuous with no. III and shows the two LBSCR lines below the three of the LCDR. Note that there were connections between the two at that time.

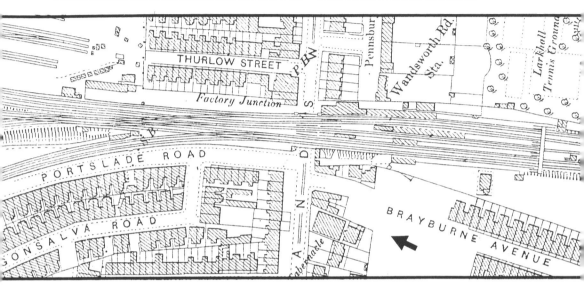

37. Three platform faces were provided for LCDR trains and were in use from 1st March 1863 until 3rd April 1916. On the extreme left are the two lines and overhead electrification equipment used by LBSCR trains. The tracks and platforms were owned by the LCDR. No. 741 was built as class D in 1902 and rebuilt to D1 in 1927. (Lens of Sutton)

38. The 2.00pm "Golden Arrow" Pullman Boat Train from Victoria to Folkestone Harbour passes Wandsworth Road on 23rd May 1953, hauled by BR "Britannia" class 4-6-2 no. 70004 *William Shakespeare*. This locomotive, regularly used on this prestigious duty and kept in pristine condition by Stewarts Lane shed staff, commenced its career as an exhibit at the 1951 "Festival of Britain". The gap between the up tracks resulted from the removal of the island platform seen in the previous picture. (N.Sprinks)

39. Working from the Eastern Region on 6th June 1953 is class J17 0-6-0 no. 65572 transferring 21 wagons from Temple Mills to Hither Green. In the distance is the incline to the high level lines and Factory Junction box. Bunting is on show for the coronation of Queen Elizabeth II. (J.J.Smith)

40. Ex-LBSCR class E2 no. 32100 is plodding along the up relief line in June 1953 carrying the Herne Hill-Stewarts Lane headcode. It is signalled to turn off at Factory Junction - this was not possible from the up main at that time. The bridge carries Larkhall Rise. (P.Hay)

41. The 15.23 Victoria to Dover Priory via Canterbury East on 8th April 1989 takes the down Chatham main line and passes over the connection laid on 30th September 1979 to allow down trains to cross from the Chatham reversible, the western track of the three on the high level route. A scheme was drawn up in 1989 to convert the redundant Battersea Power Station (background) to a leisure complex and provide an exclusive train service to Victoria. The project did not materialise at that time. (A.Dasi-Sutton)

42. Another, but eastward, view from Larkhall Rise bridge in 1989, features no.47280 with the 10.26 Dover to Mossend (Glasgow) service. Clapham station is in the distance, the wooded site on the left once accommodating its goods yard. The South London Lines are on the right. (A.Dasi-Sutton)

CLAPHAM

43. As at Wandsworth Road, the three platforms on the LCDR lines had been closed on 3rd April 1916 and subsequently demolished. However, they had come into use earlier, on 28th August 1862. Class U1 no. 31906 heads for Ramsgate with the 11.50am from Victoria on 20th April 1957. (S.C.Nash)

VI. The 1895 map reveals the extent of the goods yard which closed on 10th June 1963. The southern pair of tracks were the original LCDR main line but these were used by the LBSCR trains from 1st May 1867, by which time the three northern lines were ready.

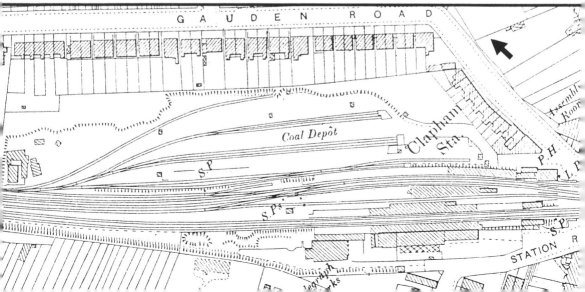

44. For some years the LSWR called the station Clapham Town, presumably to reduce confusion with Clapham Junction. This was during the period of running to Ludgate Hill.

The last working of the "Golden Arrow" was recorded on 30th September 1972, the electric locomotive being no. 5013. (J.Scrace)

45. "Schools" class no. 30938 *St. Olaves* approaches the end of the triple track section with the 2.35pm Victoria to Ramsgate train on 20th April 1957. The up relief line was used extensively by freight services. (S.C.Nash)

46. The up relief line diverged on the London side of Shepherds Lane box (centre). This 1955 photograph shows the box that was opened on 2nd November 1943, following war damage to its predecessor. A subsequent box, which also controlled the junction at Brixton, was in use from 8th March 1959 until 29th November 1981. (British Rail)

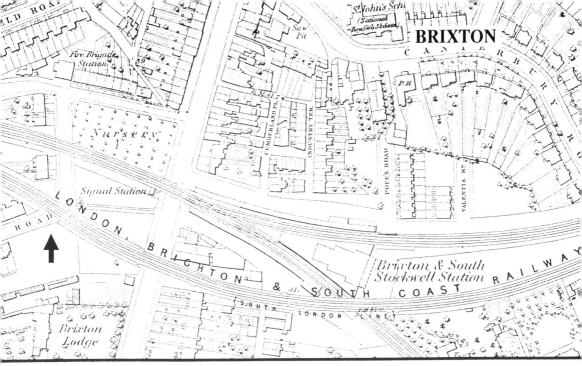

VII. The 1875 map has the lines from Victoria on the left, from Denmark Hill on the right, and from Herne Hill at the bottom. Note that many of the houses were large with spacious gardens and probably accommodated 1st class season ticket holders.

47. Ex-LSWR class T9 no. E304 enters Brixton station on 28th March 1929 bound for Ramsgate via the Catford Loop. Visible in the background is the signal box which was known as "Brixton Tower" for many years, although the map describes it as a "Signal Station". The box closed on 8th March 1959.
(H.C.Casserley)

48. An up train on 28th March 1929 passes through the Catford Loop line platforms which were taken out of use at about this time. The locomotive is F1 class no. A203 of 1885. In the background is the South London Line, which used overhead electrical supply until 17th June 1928. (H.C.Casserley)

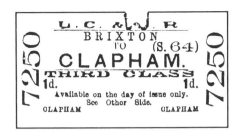

L. C. & D. R.
BRIXTON
TO (S. 64)
CLAPHAM.
THIRD CLASS
1d. 1d.
Available on the day of issue only.
See Other Side.
CLAPHAM CLAPHAM
7250 7250

49. A down Dover train passes under the South London line in the 1930s, hauled by class D1 no. 1502. This excursion is destined for Ramsgate via Herne Hill. The station had the suffix "& South Stockwell" from 1st May 1863 until 9th July 1934. Originally the entrance was in the vee of the junction, facing east as at Lewisham - see map. (Lens of Sutton)

50. The view towards Herne Hill in the 1960s had changed little in the subsequent 30 years, except that the lattice bridge was replaced by a steel structure in October 1989. This was part of a programme of bridge strengthening to allow Channel Tunnel freight trains to use the Catford Loop. (British Rail)

51. Access to the remaining up platform was (and is) via a long flight of steps. The northern pair of platforms and the staircase were largely removed in about 1930. This bridge passes over Atlantic Road as well as the South London lines which assume the name "Atlantic" in this area. (British Rail)

52. Sadly the opportunity to incorporate platforms in the new bridge for South London trains was missed, particularly as the nearby East Brixton station was closed in 1976 and an all day service on this line was restored on 13th May 1991. The bronze figures were completed in June 1986, a large number of authorities contributing to the cost. (J.Scrace)

53. A third bronze figure representing potential local passengers backs onto this one and faces the remains of the long disused second up platform. On 16th January 1991, class 411 4CEP no. 1616 curves towards Herne Hill. Facing connections from the east to the South London lines near Shepherds Lane were added in March 1991 in readiness for traffic from mainland Europe. (M.Turvey)

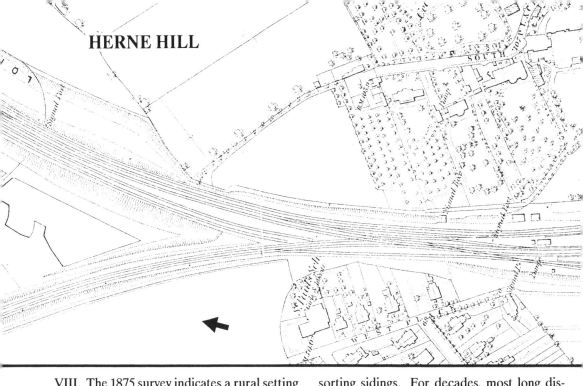

HERNE HILL

VIII. The 1875 survey indicates a rural setting with well spaced country houses. Both maps have the Victoria to Bromley South route from lower left to top right. The LCDR's City branch is top left, as are some of the Herne Hill sorting sidings. For decades, most long distance up trains were divided here for Victoria and Holborn Viaduct. Lower right is the line to Tulse Hill.

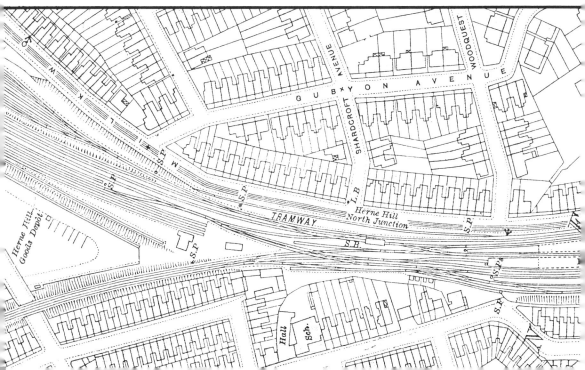

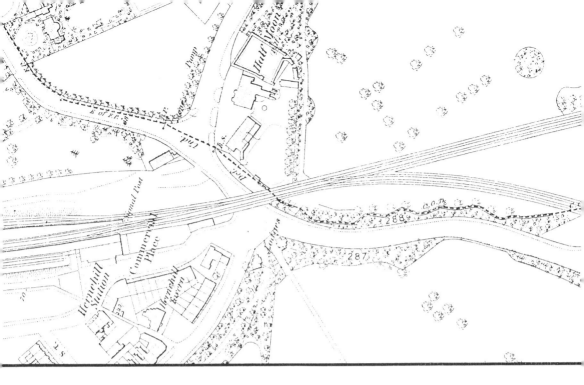

IX. By the time of the 1916 survey, the large houses had given way to terraces and the types of tickets sold no doubt altered accordingly. In 1909, electric trams commenced, both tracks running on the same side of the road past Brockwell Park, lower right. Lower right on both maps is the spur to Tulse Hill which was used almost exclusively by LSWR trains between Ludgate Hill and Wimbledon until 1st January 1917. From the mid-1860s until the mid-1890s, these trains ran through to Kingston. From August 1923 there were seven weekday services between Wimbledon and Ludgate Hill until electrification on 4th March 1929, when these were replaced by a half-hourly service to Holborn Viaduct.

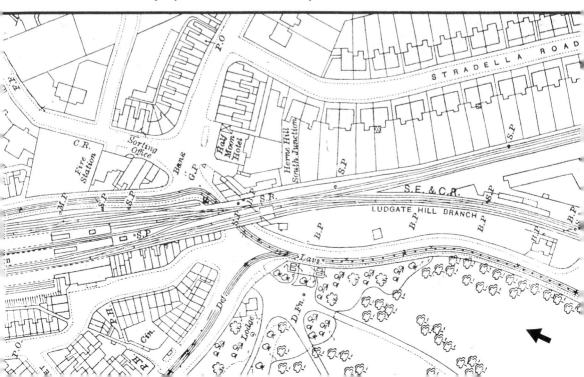

54. As at Denmark Hill (still standing) and Ludgate Hill (long gone), the LCDR built stations to impress passengers, but this was before the company's bankruptcy. This north-ward view shows that five through platform faces were provided until the rebuilding prior to electrification. The up bay platform is barely visible. (Lens of Sutton)

55. On 1st January 1866, a New Barnet - Herne Hill service commenced in conjunction with the Great Northern Railway. This up train bears the headboard *MIDLAND RAILWAY* and is probably bound for Hendon, a des-tination served by trains via Farringdon since 1st July 1875. (Lens of Sutton)

56. Class E no. A273 stands at the down island platform on 11th July 1925, the day before electric suburban services commenced, hence the clean insulators. (H.C.Casserley)

57. The 12.35 Victoria-Ramsgate train approaches Herne Hill on Maundy Thursday, 15th April 1954, hauled by ex-SR "King Arthur" class 4-6-0 no. 30766 *Sir Geraint*. The locomotive exhaust is obscuring the view of the impressive elevated North Box which controlled the junction of the lines to Victoria and Holborn Viaduct. (N.Sprinks)

58. The signalman's view from North Box ("A" Box in latter years) included part of Herne Hill Yard. The diagram shows that the two occupied sidings were for traffic to the former Midland and Great Northern lines. (D.Cullum)

Control diagram of Herne Hill Yard, showing siding lengths in feet.

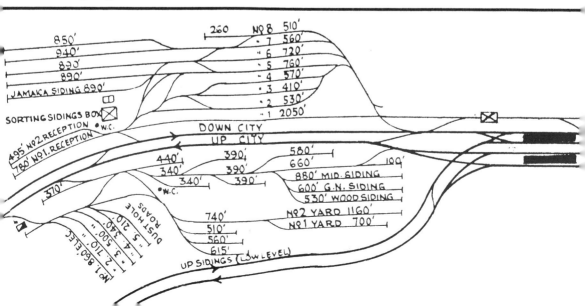

59. Another photograph from "A" Box on 26th May 1956, but looking south, shows the complexity of the trackwork in the area. In the distance is "B" Box and the tall station building. (D.Cullum)

60. Both boxes straddled the lines they controlled and were replaced by a single box on 3rd June 1956. This South or "B" Box is viewed from Norwood Road in September 1953 when an obsolete tramway section box and telephone was still in situ. (D.Cullum)

61. The original buildings, seen in 1953, were little altered by 1991. Most of the structure was converted that year to a 3000 sq ft office accommodation, known as "Tower House". Goods facilities were withdrawn on 1st August 1966. (D.Cullum)

C. & D. R.
HERNE HILL
TO
SHORTLANDS.
SECOND CLASS
9d.   9d
Available on the day of issue only.
See Other Side.
SHORTLANDS   SHORTLANDS
1417   1417

62. Two views from "B" Box in 1956 emphasise the importance of good visibility for signalmen. The track on the right was used by down freight services. Part of it was retained and electrified as a siding and was still in place in 1991 but out of use. Compare this with picture 54. (D.Cullum)

63. The main line to Bromley South is on the left and on the right is the 1 in 66 line up to Tulse Hill, built by the LCDR and opened on 1st January 1869, giving a connection with the LBSCR. Misreading a fogman's hand signal on 6th November 1947, the driver of an up Ramsgate express collided with a Holborn Viaduct to West Croydon electric on the diamond crossing. (D.Cullum)

64. The new box at the north end of the station was in use from 3rd June 1956 until 6th December 1981 and was still standing in 1991, but used by permanent way staff. This photograph dates from April 1982. (J.Scrace)

65. A 4CEP from Ramsgate speeds through platform 2 on 5th June 1990. This island platform was entirely new for the suburban electrification scheme, whereas the down one was retained in its original position. (A.C.Mott)

66. Kirtley class D no. 558 is seen at West Dulwich in SECR livery, prior to its withdrawal in 1910. Built by Neilson & Co in 1873 to Kirtley's design, the locomotive was named *Mona* and numbered 99 by the LCDR. A boiler from Longhedge Works was fitted in 1902. SER coaches were vacuum braked but the LCDR stock had air brakes, hence this engine was dual fitted, although at the rear only. (A.C.Ingram coll.)

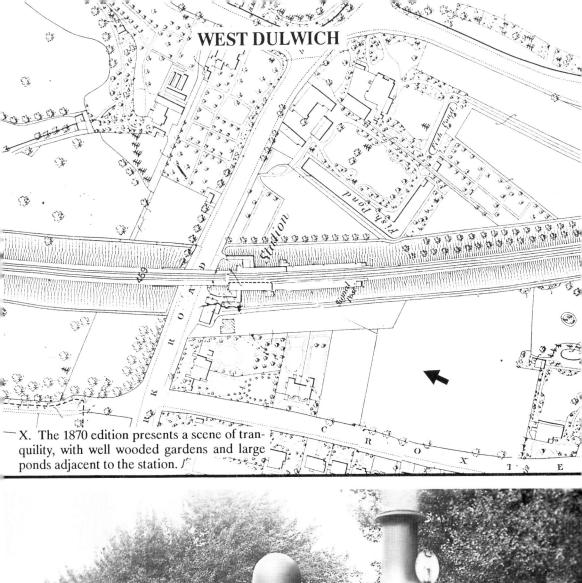

WEST DULWICH

X. The 1870 edition presents a scene of tran-
quility, with well wooded gardens and large
ponds adjacent to the station.

67. Showing an 1862 plate, the bridge design was dictated by the nearby Dulwich College Estate. A similar style was used at Lordship Lane - see picture 26 in *Crystal Palace and* *Catford Loop*. Note the regulation design cabmen's tearoom in the road.
(Lens of Sutton)

68. The structure of the bridge is evident on the inside of the ornamental railings, as class B2 SECR no. 655 approaches with a down goods. One of six 0-6-0s built for the LCDR in 1891, this engine was originally numbered 196.
(Lens of Sutton)

69. The station first appeared in timetables in October 1863, as Dulwich. "West" was added on 20th September 1926, North Dulwich and East Dulwich already having prefixes. Two views from September 1952 show platform improvements in progress. Note the additional gas light for the running-in board. (D.Cullum)

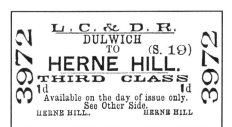

Main Line freight services in 1892

Down		Up	
am		**am**	
12.20	Battersea - Dover Priory	1.00	Queenborough Pier - Blackfriars
12.50	Queenborough Pier - Canterbury (Coal)	6.15	Queenborough Pier - Battersea
1.15	Blackfriars - Ashford	**pm**	
1.40	Blackfriars - Maidstone	1.20	Faversham - Battersea
2.00	Battersea - Dover Harbour	4.25	Dover Priory - Blackfriars
2.30	Battersea - Gravesend	4.45	Sittingbourne - Battersea
3.15	Battersea - Sevenoaks	6.00	Sevenoaks - Battersea
3.45	Blackfriars - Queenborough Pier	6.15	Ashford - Blackfriars
4.45	Herne Hill - Strood	7.00	Maidstone - Blackfriars
7.18	Battersea - Sittingbourne	7.15	Gravesend - Battersea
11.15	Battersea - Faversham	7.25	Ramsgate - Blackfriars
pm		8.05	Dover Harbour - Blackfriars
12.10	Battersea - Maidstone	8.25	Ashford - Battersea
5.40	Battersea - Queenborough Pier	9.10	Maidstone - Battersea
9.00	Battersea - Faversham	11.00	Queenborough Pier - Blackfriars
11.20	Battersea - Ramsgate		

70. The down platform (right) was rebuilt again on concrete piers in the 1980s, the up one having been reconstructed on a steel structure. Embankment instability is the cause of continual platform movement here. (D.Cullum)

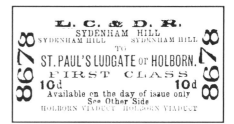

71. The roadside offices are seen in about 1960. Although boarded up in 1991, the booking office was still in use during the morning. At other times access to the up platform was via the path on the right and a long covered way. (British Rail)

72. On 10th August 1990, the 13.50 Victoria to Ramsgate rushes east, the "Jaffa cake" livery having just disappeared from these class 411 units. Beyond the projecting train indicators, a staff room was retained in part of the old buildings. Here hand written tickets could be obtained during the afternoon. (J.Scrace)

WEST OF SYDENHAM HILL

73. Alleyn Park road bridge had ornate railings and kerbside columns until attacked by the enemy airforce on 15th September 1940. The ornamentation demanded by Dulwich College was similar to that seen in pictures 67 and 68, it having been blasted away from the main girders. (British Rail)

74. Viewed from Union Road (now renamed Hunts Slip Road), a down train approaches Sydenham Hill. Open conductors (uninsulated wire) and porcelain insulators could enhance railway photographs, if in the background. (Lens of Sutton)

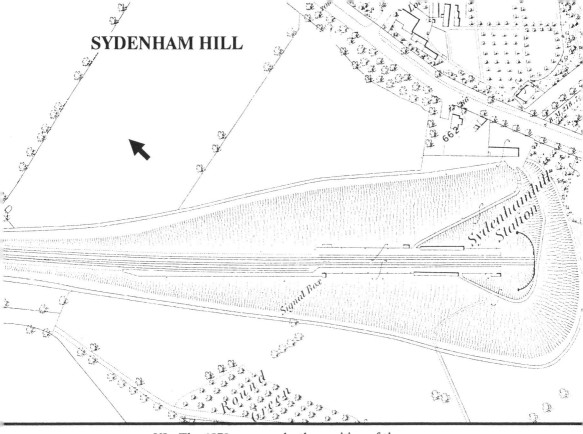

SYDENHAM HILL

XI. The 1870 map marks the position of the footpaths to each platform and the location of the first signal box.

75. The frugal LCDR shelter on the down side is evident, as is the gate from the footpath and the original signal box. LCDR no. 17 was a class M3 4-4-0, built at Longhedge Works in 1894 and renumbered 476 in 1899. (Lens of Sutton)

76. The simple economical signal box amazingly had no windows at the platform end and no stovepipe is visible. Note the external bell and convenient convenience, then known as a "privy". (G.Metherell)

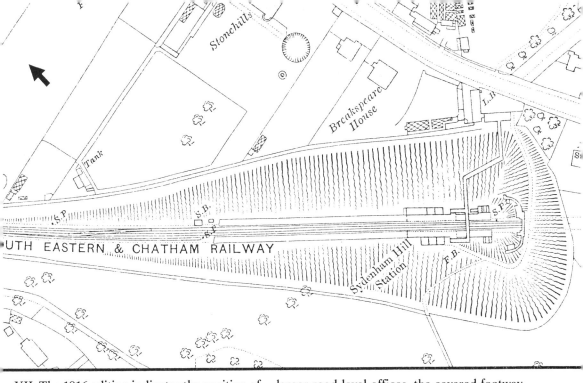

On the map: Stonehills, Breakspeare House, Tank, SOUTH EASTERN & CHATHAM RAILWAY, Sydenham Hill Station, S.B., S.P., L.B., F.B.

XII. The 1916 edition indicates the position of the longer platforms, the new signal box, the larger road level offices, the covered footway and footbridge.

77. A 1922 view towards the tunnel includes the "parsonage" above it and the copper trimmed spire of St. Stephen's church. In its early years the station was described as "for Crystal Palace", which was half a mile distant. (H.J.Patterson Rutherford)

78.   Hunts Slip Road bridge is in the background as Wainwright D class no. A577 passes Sydenham Hill's only siding. There was no road access to it, its function being to serve the engineers, or as a lay-by into which defective vehicles could be shunted and left. The train is destined for Dover via Chatham.
(Lens of Sutton)

79. H class 0-4-4T no. A320 reaches the top of the 1 in 101 climb from Herne Hill with a train of ageing six-wheelers. Note the spectacle shade, added to prevent the setting sun giving a wrong indication. The headcode indicates the Maidstone East route. (Lens of Sutton)

80. The small signal was a repeater for the indistinct distant signal inside the tunnel. Here was situated one of the first electrically operated signals, coming into use on 19th August 1875. The lining for the 2200 yd long Penge Tunnel required 33m bricks, most of them being made from clay dug from the bore. The down platform was unusual in not having a ramp at the tunnel end, a feature retained in 1991. (S.A.W.Harvey/R.C.Riley coll.)

81. The down side buildings were destroyed by arsonists in August 1981 but in 1988 the up side was improved with a new roof overall and a new booking hall at the bottom of the covered footbridge. (J.Scrace)

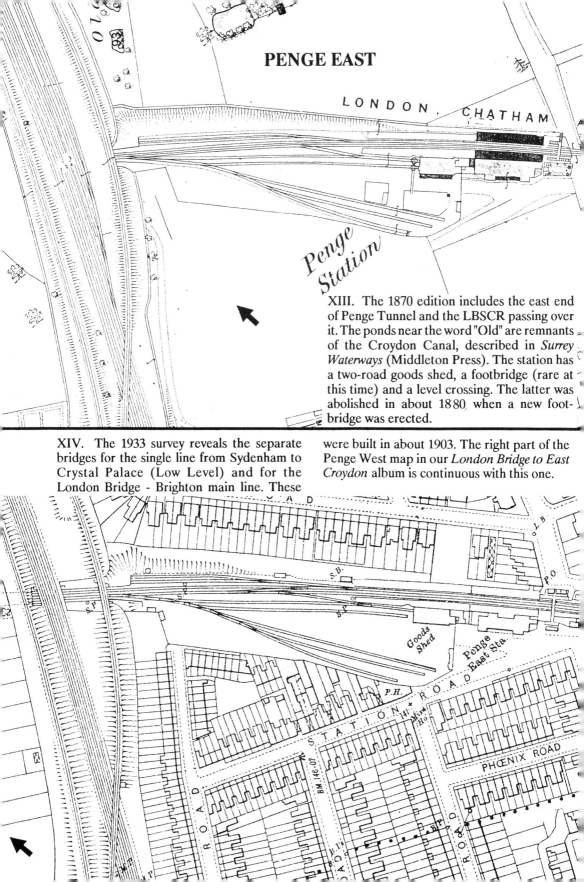

PENGE EAST

L O N D O N , C H A T H A M

Penge Station

XIII. The 1870 edition includes the east end of Penge Tunnel and the LBSCR passing over it. The ponds near the word "Old" are remnants of the Croydon Canal, described in *Surrey Waterways* (Middleton Press). The station has a two-road goods shed, a footbridge (rare at this time) and a level crossing. The latter was abolished in about 1880, when a new foot-bridge was erected.

XIV. The 1933 survey reveals the separate bridges for the single line from Sydenham to Crystal Palace (Low Level) and for the London Bridge - Brighton main line. These were built in about 1903. The right part of the Penge West map in our *London Bridge to East Croydon* album is continuous with this one.

Goods Shed

Penge East Sta.

P.H.

S T A T I O N   R O A D

BM.146·07

PHŒNIX ROAD

R O A D

Penge Railway Station.

82. A postcard view of the south elevation shows that the directors of the LCDR considered that Penge justified this substantial and impressive station, which opened with the line on 1st July 1863. The goods shed is on the left. (Lens of Sutton)

83. Looking towards London, we see the position of the second signal box, the first being close to the level crossing. The suffix "East" was added on 9th July 1923. (Lens of Sutton)

84. A westward view from about 1933 includes part of the goods yard, which was in use until 7th November 1966. The box closed on 25th February 1968. The locomotive is "King Arthur" class no. 793 *Sir Ontzlake*. (S.A.W.Harvey)

85. The second footbridge was built on the site of the level crossing and the platforms were extended. On the left is the former crossing keeper's house, which was still in place in 1991, as were the platform canopies. (S.A.W.Harvey)

86. The intricate polychromatic brickwork and the tapered chimney bases give a special and attractive charm. The slit window at half height on the house gives distinction. Recorded about 30 years ago, the building still retains its dignity. (Lens of Sutton)

87. Two class 411 units emerge from Penge Tunnel on 16th January 1991, bound for Dover. The high bridge in the background carries the line to Crystal Palace, the low one beyond it being for the four tracks of the Brighton main line. The rail mounted tractors carry flail cutters for attacking lineside vegetation. (M.Turvey)

KENT HOUSE

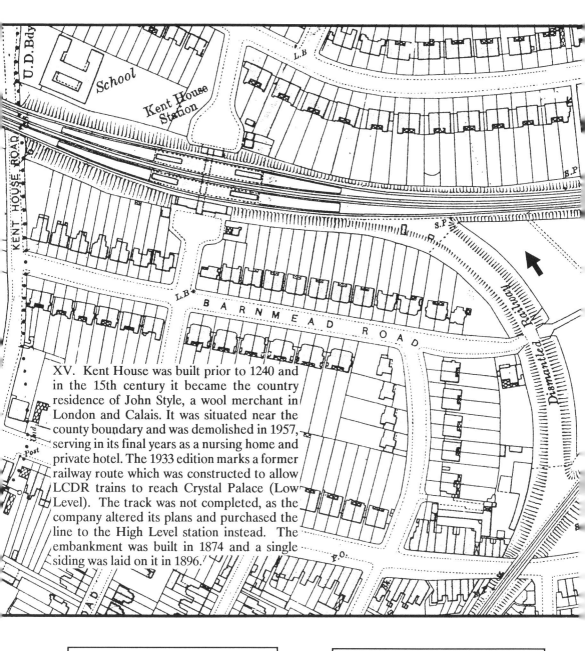

XV. Kent House was built prior to 1240 and in the 15th century it became the country residence of John Style, a wool merchant in London and Calais. It was situated near the county boundary and was demolished in 1957, serving in its final years as a nursing home and private hotel. The 1933 edition marks a former railway route which was constructed to allow LCDR trains to reach Crystal Palace (Low Level). The track was not completed, as the company altered its plans and purchased the line to the High Level station instead. The embankment was built in 1874 and a single siding was laid on it in 1896.

SOUTHERN RAILWAY.
This ticket is issued subject to the Company's Bye-laws, Regulations and Conditions in their Time Tables, Notices and Book of Regulations.

Kent House to

Kent House   Kent House
Penge East   Penge East

PENGE EAST

THIRD CLASS   THIRD CLASS
Fare 1½d.   Fare 1½d.

0220

L.C.&D.R.
KENT HOUSE (Beckenham)
KENT HOUSE   KENT HOUSE
TO   (S &c)

PENGE

SECOND CLASS
1½d.   1½d.
Available on the day of issue only.
See other Side.
PENGE   PENGE

7531

88. Class R1 0-4-4T no. 700 heads a down train and leaves the double track section from Penge. Half a mile of quadruple track was brought into use on 10th May 1886 in an attempt to reduce congestion on this increasingly busy route. (Lens of Sutton)

89. The station did not open until 1st October 1884, hence its different architectural style. Much of the land was given by Mr. Cator, a local landowner who stood to gain from development of his estate. This took place but the road outside the station was still privately owned and unsurfaced in 1991. By then there was direct access to the subway (in the gabled section), the awning had gone but the building was otherwise complete. (Lens of Sutton)

90. A down train rounds the 40-chain curve on a falling gradient of 1 in 102. There were once three signal boxes but these were eliminated in 1928-31. The buildings on the right have also gone but the down platforms retained much of their canopy and both sets of stairs to the subway in 1991. (Lens of Sutton)

91. "King Arthur" class no. 771 *Sir Sagramore* heads towards London with a Continental express and passes that part of the building which remained standing until early 1990, when vandals destroyed it by fire. Gas lights prevail despite the use of electricity for traction. (S.A.W.Harvey/R.C.Riley coll.)

92. A July 1990 view includes an up train, the end of the main buildings (now flats), and the last of the timber clad platform buildings, which contained the waiting room and staff room. (J.Scrace)

XVI. "Kent House" is top left on this 6" to 1 mile map from the early 1870s. Kent House station was built near the words "Kenthouse Lane" (left). The line below this is to Crystal Palace. From top to bottom is the SER's route from Lewisham to Croydon (now Addiscombe). From 1st January 1857 until 1st April 1864 this line terminated at Beckenham Junction (right). The station marked "closed" was in use from April 1864 until October 1866, when New Beckenham was resited north of the junction.

BECKENHAM JUNCTION

93. In the background is the overall roof, which was removed in 1890. Following the arrival of the railway the population growth was dramatic. From 2100 in 1861 it nearly trebled to 6000 in 1871 and more than doubled again in the next ten years to 13000. The station was worked by the LCDR and SER jointly. (R.C.Riley coll.)

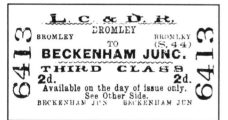

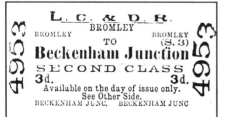

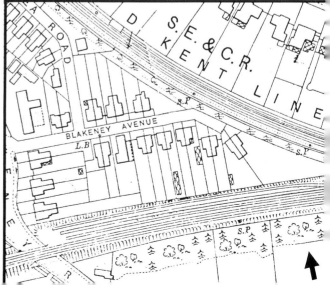

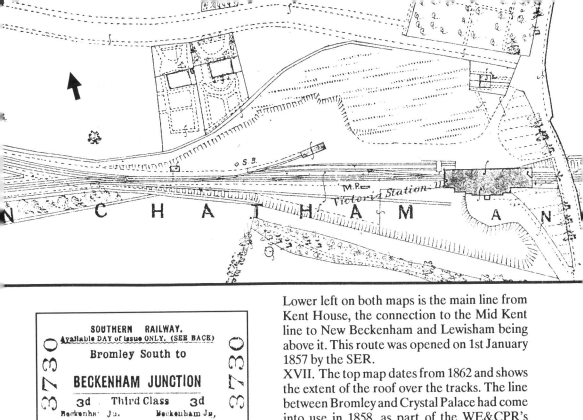

Lower left on both maps is the main line from Kent House, the connection to the Mid Kent line to New Beckenham and Lewisham being above it. This route was opened on 1st January 1857 by the SER.

XVII. The top map dates from 1862 and shows the extent of the roof over the tracks. The line between Bromley and Crystal Palace had come into use in 1858, as part of the WE&CPR's Farnborough extension.

XVIII. The bottom map is from 1912 and indicates the maximum extent of the two goods yards, together with the berthing sidings, lower left. Extensive track alterations in 1928-29 resulted in separate parallel pairs of running lines being provided west of the station, to segregate trains for Crystal Palace and Norwood Junction from the main line. The goods yard south of the station was closed and two electrified berthing sidings laid on the site.

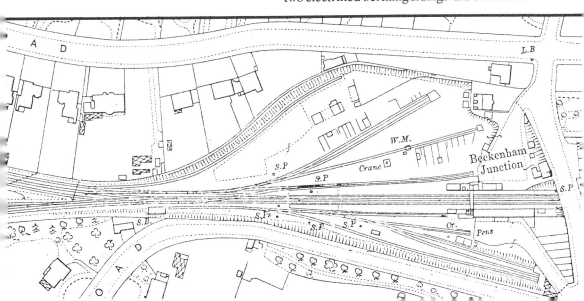

94. Pictured on 19th August 1903, class M2 4-4-0 no. 644 approaches with a down train. The distinctive SECR water columns and tapered signal arms are much in evidence. A shuttle service to Norwood Junction was operated at this time. (D.Cullum coll.)

95. The main value of this photograph is that it shows the southern goods yard prior to its closure in about 1928. Both yards had cranes - by 1938, the crane capacity was recorded as 10 tons. Goods facilities were withdrawn on 18th April 1964. (Lens of Sutton)

96. H class 0-4-4T no. A328 stands in the down bay with set 405 on 27th February 1926, the last day before electrification of Charing Cross - Hayes services. Until then there were only a few peak hour journeys on the branch from New Beckenham but thereafter a half hourly service from Cannon Street was provided. (H.C.Casserley)

BECKENHAM JUNCTION and NORWOOD JUNCTION and SOUTH NORWOOD.
London, Brighton, and South Coast and South Eastern and Chatham.

Miles.		Week Days only.							Miles.		Week Days only.						
		mrn	mrn	aft	aft	aft	aft	aft			mrn	mrn	aft	aft	aft	aft	aft
	Beckenham Junction .....|235 dep.	9 22	1148	3 32	3 24	1 37	5 7	4 5	8 30		Norwood Jn. & South Norwood dep.	8 25	1120	12 5	1 52	3 20	4 40	7 22	8 17 8 45 ....
2¼	Norwood Junc. ‡ 186, 200, 214 to arr.	9 28	1153	3 38	3 37	4 20	7 10	7 50	8 35	2¼	Beckenham Junc. 278, 280, 285. arr.	8 30	1125	1210	1 57	3 25	4 45	7 27	8 24 8 50 ....

‡ Norwood Junction and South Norwood ; station for Woodside.

October 1911 timetable. The route was operated jointly by the LBSCR and the LCDR/SECR from 18th June 1862 until 1st January 1917. For some time around 1910 the regular locomotive was class P 0-6-0T no. 323, now named *Bluebell*. Freight continued over the spur until 11th September 1959 and it closed on 30th October 1966.

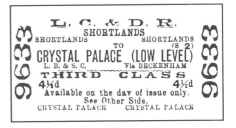

L. C. & D. R.
SHORTLANDS
SHORTLANDS   SHORTLANDS (8 2)
TO
CRYSTAL PALACE (LOW LEVEL)
L. B. & S. C.   Via BECKENHAM
THIRD   CLASS
4½d   4½d
Available on the day of issue only.
See Other Side.
CRYSTAL PALACE   CRYSTAL PALACE
9633   9633

97. Intended to show the up starting signals in 1949, this photograph also includes the goods yard, the cattle pens, and the down bay starting signals. The positions of the signals confirm that trains could leave simultaneously from the up main and up bay platforms, the latter routed via Birkbeck. (D.Cullum)

98. "Next stop Birkbeck". The 2.6pm Victoria via Crystal Palace, formed of two 2NOL units, leaves the up bay on 30th December 1956. This track was electrified on 3rd March 1929. On the left class O1 no. 31048 leaves for London Bridge via the Mid Kent line with a railtour bearing the headboard "Mid Kent Rly. and WE&CP Rly. Centenarian". (S.C.Nash)

2nd · SINGLE		SINGLE · 2nd
Brixton to		
Beckenham Jc.		Beckenham Jc.
BECKENHAM JUNCTION		
Via Kent House		
(S)	1/- FARE 1/-	(S)
For conditions see over		For conditions see over

99. On the left is the up connection to the Birkbeck line, the down connection being further west. The signal box is seen on 20th April 1958 as its successor is being erected. This came into use on 12th April 1959 and closed on 13th April 1983. It was identical to Shortlands Junction box, shown in picture 104. The spur to New Beckenham is on the right. (A.E.Bennett)

100.   Approaching platform 3 on 5th April 1987 is no. 47628 *Sir Daniel Gooch* with the 09.45 (Sundays only) Reading to Dover service. Later the 09.03 Wolverhampton to Dover would speed through, both trains only calling at Bromley South between their Kensington and Ashford stops. Both services were withdrawn in the following month. (J.Petley)

101.   Stopping trains to Victoria stand in both bay platforms on 10th August 1990. The EPB on the left will run on the route of this book while no. 5871 will travel via Crystal Palace, not Norbury as indicated. Combined with main line departures, Beckenham benefits from an excellent train service. (J.Scrace)

SHORTLANDS JUNCTION

SOUTHERN RAILWAY.
Issued subject to the Bye-laws, Regulations &
Conditions in the Company's Bills and Notices.
Herne Hill to
Herne Hill — Herne Hill
Orpington — Orpington
ORPINGTON
6507
THIRD CLASS — THIRD CLASS
Fare 1/9 — Fare 1/9
NOT TRANSFERABLE.

SOUTHERN RAILWAY.
Kent House to
Kent House — Kent House
Shortlands — Shortlands
SHORTLANDS
0993
THIRD CLASS — THIRD CLASS
Fare 4d. — Fare 4d.
FOR CONDITIONS SEE BACK

102. Class N no. 31854 approaches Shortlands Box on 2nd August 1958, when new track was being laid. The box was on the north side of the tracks and did not carry the word "junction". (R.C.Riley)

103. An up express approaches the junction on the same day, hauled by N class no. 31411. The new line in the foreground allowed Victoria - bound trains to pass by the junction unimpeded. Until May 1959 the quadruple track eastwards was arranged so that adjacent pairs of lines carried trains in the same direction. (R.C.Riley)

104. A new signal box came into use on 31st May 1959 just prior to the electrification of the lines to Ramsgate and Dover. The Catford Loop lines pass behind the box, which ceased to function on 20th June 1982 when the Victoria Panel took control of the area. In 1991, the building was in use by permanent way staff. The sub-station housed rotary converters for the 1925 electrification. (J.Scrace)

SHORTLANDS

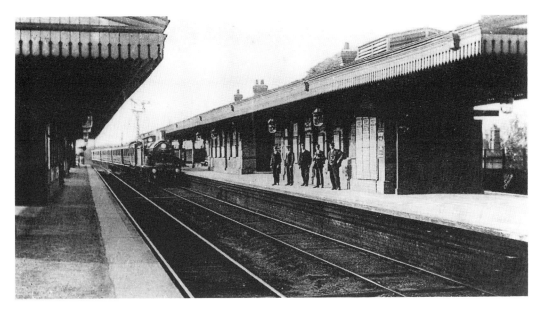

105. The station was a temporary terminus between 3rd May and 5th July 1858, when the line to Bickley (then Southborough Road) was completed. These platforms were completed ready for the operation of quadruple track from 1st May 1894. This shows the down island platform. (Lens of Sutton)

XIX. The 1863 edition marks the tiny station surrounded by fields.

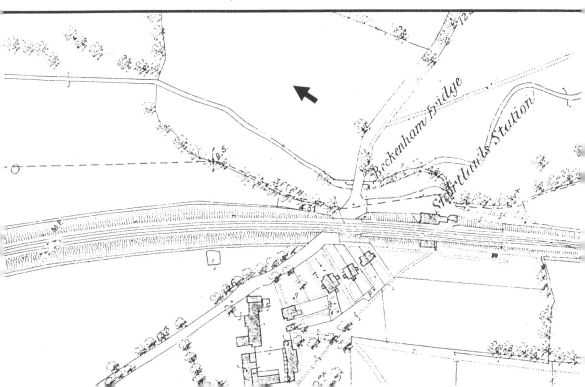

106. A fine photograph from August 1911 features E class 4-4-0 no. 547 running towards the bridge built in 1892. This train carried coaches from Manchester (via Kensington), from Kings Cross (via Ludgate Hill) and from Bradford (via Kentish Town and Ludgate Hill). They were combined at Herne Hill and ran to Dover Harbour via Folkestone. At that time distant signals showed red or green instead of the now familiar yellow or green aspects. To distinguish them at night a white illuminated fish tail (the Coligny-Welch indicator) was added. (H.J. Patterson Rutherford coll.)

107. The down "Granville Express" to
Ramsgate, complete with carriage roofboards,
is hauled by class M3 no. 647. Just visible on
the left is the roof of Shortlands Station signal
box, which was abolished on 20th December
1925. (A.C.Ingram coll.)

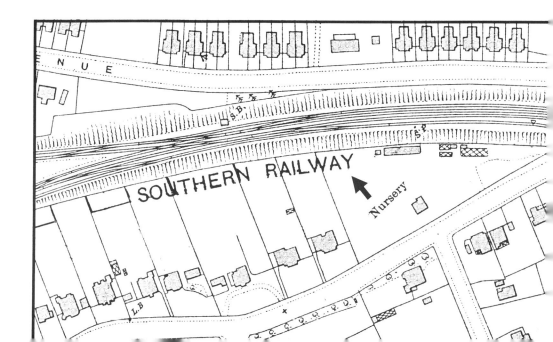

108. Shortlands was an excellent location to observe and record locomotives at work. A fine clear exhaust commends the fireman of class L no. 1776 on this Victoria - Ramsgate train in 1938. (C.R.L.Coles)

XX. The 1933 survey shows residential development complete in the station area and Shortlands Junction on the left.

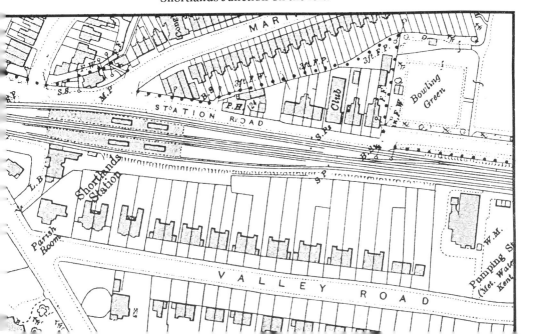

109. The station buildings are at a right angle to the track and are seen in about 1960. Insufficient car park space resulted in the station master's garden (right) and his house being cleared away. (British Rail)

110. Showing the 1959 revised track layout, no. 73138 hauls the Venice Simplon Orient Express through Shortlands on 3rd January 1987. The headcode 42 indicated that it would take the Maidstone East route to the coast. (J.Petley)

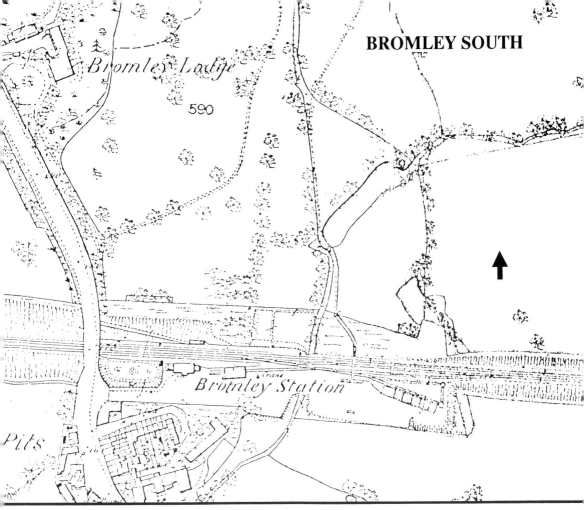

XXI. Bromley's first station was situated in the country, remote from the small market town. This 1863 map shows the main building to be south of the line.

111. This early view towards London reveals that no footbridge was provided between the platforms but that an elaborate one with two flights at the south end was erected for a public footpath. Everything was swept away prior to the quadrupling in 1893-94. (D.Cullum coll.)

112. An eastward view from the public footbridge in July 1921 features a special train arriving behind class M3 4-4-0 no.485, built at Longhedge Works in 1900. The coal yard was almost deserted owing to the season.
(H.J. Patterson Rutherford)

SOUTHERN RAILWAY.
Issued subject to the Bye-laws, Regulations &
Conditions in the Company's Bills and Notices.
Shortlands to
Shortlands   Shortlands
Bromley South   Bromley South
BROMLEY SOUTH
THIRD CLASS   THIRD CLASS
Fare 2d.   Fare 2d.
NOT TRANSFERABLE.
5812   5812

S. E. & C. & D. RYS.
Available Date of issue only. See back.
BROMLEY SOUTH
BROMLEY   BROMLEY
TO   (8.56)
BECKENHAM JUNC.
THIRD CLASS
2d   2d
BECKENHAM JUN   BECKENHAM JUN
5485   5485

113. "South" has been added to the nameboard. This was done on 1st June 1899, following the formation of the SECR. Bromley North is featured in our *Charing Cross to Orpington* album. No. A197, a class F1 4-4-0, stands adjacent to the dock road on 24th February 1931. (H.C.Casserley)

114. Difficult conditions prevailed on Christmas Eve 1938 as passengers made good use of the canopies during heavy snowfalls. The two 3SUB units were bound for Orpington. One dot over the letter was used on Victoria services and two for Holborn Viaduct. (H.C.Casserley)

115. Rucksacks were in evidence on 19th April 1953 as no. 34071 *601 Squadron* arrives with a ramblers' excursion to Lenham. On the left is 4SUB no. 4748, one of a batch introduced in 1948 for suburban work and which were in service until 1983. (D.Cullum)

116. Track work was in progress on 20th October 1957 and the cutting had been widened in preparation for the Kent Coast electrification scheme, which involved track realignment and raising the speed limit to 60 mph. However, not all of the levelled ground was used. (Pamlin Prints)

117. Prior to the commencement of electric services to the Kent Coast, platform lengthening was necessary. This is the scene on 21st March 1959. The signal box closed on 31st May of that year but the public footbridge remained. (D.Cullum)

118. Without major engineering work, only small station buildings can be built on bridges, hence this modest structure, seen in about 1960. In the thirty years from 1861 to 1891, the population almost quadrupled from about 5500 to over 21,000, due to the good railway service provided. The drawings for this building were dated 1893. (British Rail)

119. The 14.40 Dover Western Docks to Victoria on 6th October 1986 was headed by MLV no. 68005. These motor luggage vans were little used by 1991, some latterly having been used for mail traffic. Part of the siding remained in situ in 1992 but was little used. (J.Scrace)

Other photographs and maps of Shortlands and Bromley South appear in our *Crystal Palace and Catford Loop* album.

120. The 09.11 Cricklewood to Orpington approaches Bromley South on 12th November 1988. Thameslink services to destinations north of the Thames commenced in May 1988, helping to give Bromley its best ever rail service. (C.Wilson)

MP Middleton Press

Easebourne Lane, Midhurst. West Sussex. GU29 9AZ
(0730) 813169
Write or telephone for our latest booklist

BRANCH LINES

BRANCH LINES TO MIDHURST
BRANCH LINES AROUND MIDHURST
BRANCH LINES TO HORSHAM
BRANCH LINE TO SELSEY
BRANCH LINES TO EAST GRINSTEAD
BRANCH LINES TO ALTON
BRANCH LINE TO TENTERDEN
BRANCH LINES TO NEWPORT
BRANCH LINES TO TUNBRIDGE WELLS
BRANCH LINE TO SWANAGE
BRANCH LINE TO LYME REGIS
BRANCH LINE TO FAIRFORD
BRANCH LINE TO ALLHALLOWS
BRANCH LINES AROUND ASCOT
BRANCH LINES AROUND WEYMOUTH
BRANCH LINE TO HAWKHURST
BRANCH LINES AROUND EFFINGHAM JN
BRANCH LINE TO MINEHEAD
BRANCH LINE TO SHREWSBURY
BRANCH LINES AROUND HUNTINGDON
BRANCH LINES TO SEATON AND SIDMOUTH
BRANCH LINES AROUND WIMBORNE

SOUTH COAST RAILWAYS

CHICHESTER TO PORTSMOUTH
BRIGHTON TO EASTBOURNE
RYDE TO VENTNOR
EASTBOURNE TO HASTINGS
PORTSMOUTH TO SOUTHAMPTON
HASTINGS TO ASHFORD
SOUTHAMPTON TO BOURNEMOUTH
ASHFORD TO DOVER
BOURNEMOUTH TO WEYMOUTH
DOVER TO RAMSGATE

SOUTHERN MAIN LINES

HAYWARDS HEATH TO SEAFORD
EPSOM TO HORSHAM
CRAWLEY TO LITTLEHAMPTON
THREE BRIDGES TO BRIGHTON
WATERLOO TO WOKING
VICTORIA TO EAST CROYDON
EAST CROYDON TO THREE BRIDGES
WOKING TO SOUTHAMPTON
WATERLOO TO WINDSOR
LONDON BRIDGE TO EAST CROYDON
BASINGSTOKE TO SALISBURY
SITTINGBOURNE TO RAMSGATE
YEOVIL TO EXETER
CHARING CROSS TO ORPINGTON

COUNTRY RAILWAY ROUTES

BOURNEMOUTH TO EVERCREECH JN
READING TO GUILDFORD
WOKING TO ALTON
BATH TO EVERCREECH JUNCTION
GUILDFORD TO REDHILL
EAST KENT LIGHT RAILWAY
FAREHAM TO SALISBURY
BURNHAM TO EVERCREECH JUNCTION
REDHILL TO ASHFORD
YEOVIL TO DORCHESTER
ANDOVER TO SOUTHAMPTON

LONDON SUBURBAN RAILWAYS

CHARING CROSS TO DARTFORD
HOLBORN VIADUCT TO LEWISHAM
KINGSTON & HOUNSLOW LOOPS
CRYSTAL PALACE AND CATFORD LOOP
LEWISHAM TO DARTFORD

STEAMING THROUGH

STEAMING THROUGH EAST HANTS
STEAMING THROUGH SURREY
STEAMING THROUGH WEST SUSSEX
STEAMING THROUGH THE ISLE OF WIGHT
STEAMING THROUGH WEST HANTS

OTHER RAILWAY BOOKS

GARRAWAY FATHER & SON
LONDON CHATHAM & DOVER RAILWAY
INDUSTRIAL RAILWAYS OF THE S. EAST
WEST SUSSEX RAILWAYS IN THE 1980s
SOUTH EASTERN RAILWAY

OTHER BOOKS

WALKS IN THE WESTERN HIGH WEALD
TILLINGBOURNE BUS STORY

MILITARY DEFENCE OF WEST SUSSEX
BATTLE OVER SUSSEX 1940

SURREY WATERWAYS
KENT AND EAST SUSSEX WATERWAYS
HAMPSHIRE WATERWAYS